The STICK MAN
Sticker Activity Book

By Julia Donaldson

Illustrated by Axel Scheffler

ALISON GREEN BOOKS

Spot the Difference

Can you spot ten differences between
these two snowy scenes?

Stick Man is Lost!

Can you help Stick Man find the right
path back to the family tree?

Stick Man's Wordsearch

There are ten words hidden in this wordsearch. One has already been circled for you – can you find the other nine?

BAT

STICK

KNIGHT
(already circled)

ARM

A	F	L	H	O	O	K	D	I	S
R	D	X	N	E	A	N	K	Q	T
M	P	L	G	T	W	I	G	J	L
C	O	V	S	I	H	G	L	F	P
M	B	O	W	U	Y	H	R	L	Z
P	A	F	R	P	Z	T	O	A	O
B	O	O	M	E	R	A	N	G	K
A	R	O	G	N	P	F	E	O	N
T	P	H	O	U	Y	O	F	Y	X
P	D	G	P	F	S	T	I	C	K

TWIG

HOOK

BOW

FLAG   BOOMERANG   PEN

Ho-Ho-Ho!

Look who's just come down the chimney!
Can you colour in Santa in his festive red suit?

Floating Down the River

There are three pieces missing from this jigsaw.
Can you find them in the sticker section and
complete the scene? You could even add more
stickers to decorate the page.

Sticker Scene

Who's playing in the snow?

These are the stickers for 'What's Next?'

These are the stickers for the 'Floating Down the River' Jigsaw

School Time

Can you help the Stick Children with their lessons?

Can you count the birds?

Can you do the sums?

$2 + 2 =$

$3 - 2 =$

$4 + 1 =$

Can you work out who is who by matching the fragment to their whole picture?

Can you match the pairs?

Can you spot the odd one out?

Can you match the colours to the pictures on the right?

YELLOW GREY GREEN BLUE RED

Fun at the Beach

Can you colour in this sunny scene?

Splish, Splash!

Who's this paddling on the river? Join the dots to find out.

Drawing Fun

Draw the characters by copying each square of
the top grid into the blank grid on the bottom.

What's Next?

Find the right sticker in the sticker section to
complete each of the patterns below.

Answers

Spot the Difference

Stick Man is Lost!

Stick Man's Wordsearch

A	F	L	H	O	O	K	D	I	S
R	D	X	N	E	A	N	K	Q	T
M	P	L	G	T	W	I	G	J	L
C	O	V	S	I	H	G	L	F	P
M	B	O	W	U	Y	H	R	L	Z
P	A	F	R	P	Z	T	O	A	O
B	O	O	M	E	R	A	N	G	K
A	R	O	G	N	P	F	E	O	N
T	P	H	O	U	Y	O	F	Y	X
P	D	G	P	F	S	T	I	C	K

School Time

Can you count the birds?

4

$$2 + 2 = 4$$
$$3 - 2 = 1$$
$$4 + 1 = 5$$

Can you spot the odd one out?

What's Next?